Alan Bowness

GAUGUIN

Φ

Phaidon

Phaidon Press Limited, 5 Cromwell Place, London SW7 2JL

First published 1971
Second edition 1972
Reprinted 1975

© *1972 by Phaidon Press Limited*

ISBN 0 7148 1579 9

Printed in Italy

GAUGUIN

MORE THAN WITH MOST PAINTERS, the shape of Gauguin's turbulent career was predetermined by his heredity and early environment. The popular idea of the successful business man who suddenly and surprisingly decided to be a painter could scarcely be further from the truth. What is more remarkable indeed is how closely the art which Gauguin created and which was to have such a widespread influence responded to his private needs. His life and work were dominated by the feeling that he must somehow recapture a lost paradise dimly remembered from early childhood. Unable to find it, he remade it in his own art, but only at the cost of self-destruction. The drama was played out over little more than twenty years, against a background of the most momentous changes in the history of art since the Renaissance. And although he may not have been the greatest artist involved, his contribution was arguably the major one.

Eugène-Henri-Paul Gauguin was born in Paris on 7th June 1848, at the most violent phase of the 1848 Revolution – a propitious enough moment. His father, Clovis Gauguin, was a 34-year-old journalist, who worked for a liberal newspaper that was soon to be suppressed. Clovis came from Orléans, and there is nothing in the Gauguin family history of market gardeners and small business men to suggest an artistic temperament.

With Clovis's wife, Aline-Marie Chazal, it is a very different matter, however. She was only 22 when her son was born, and already had a one-year-old daughter, Marie, Paul's only sibling. Aline was the daughter of André Chazal, engraver, and of Flora Tristan, author and social reformer. Theirs had been an ill-matched, short-lived marriage; it culminated in Chazal attempting to murder his wife and being sentenced to twenty years' imprisonment.

Paul owed much to this tempestuous pair. Flora Tristan was the illegitimate daughter of a young woman, Thérèse Laisnay, of whose background nothing whatever is known. She seems to have fled to Spain at the French Revolution, though whether she was an aristocrat or an adventuress, it is impossible to say. In Bilbao she became the mistress of a well connected Spanish colonel of Dragoons, Don Mariano de Tristan Moscoso. They moved to Paris where Flora was born in 1803: the liason was a stable one, but Don Mariano died suddenly before bringing himself to marry his mistress. This catapulted her from luxury to penury, and the rest of her miserable life was spent pleading the claims for herself and her daughter.

She had grounds for feeling that she was owed something. The Tristan Moscoso family belonged to the old Aragonese nobility, and were among the early Spanish settlers in Peru, where they had become powerful and extremely wealthy. Gauguin liked to believe that they had intermarried with the Inca aristocracy, and this is certainly possible. Don Mariano's brother, Don Pio, took part in the early nineteenth century War of Peruvian Independence, and was Viceroy for a time. It was to him that Flora, having deserted her dull husband, appealed. He agreed to make a small allowance to his niece, and thus encouraged, Flora set sail for Peru, in the hopes that a personal appeal would bring her a larger share of the considerable family fortune.

She was wrong, but a by-product of her South American trip was the book, *Pérégrinations d'une Paria* (*Wanderings of an outcast*). Published in 1838, this made Flora Tristan's literary reputation, and launched her in the world of letters. She wrote a novel, but soon turned to social reform and espoused the revolutionary working class movements of the day. Followed by police spies, she travelled France addressing meetings of the urban proletariat whom she called upon to unite. Physically exhausted by such activities, she collapsed and died in Bordeaux in November 1844, less than four years before the revolution of 1848 to which she had made such a signal contribution. Paul Gauguin idolized his grandmother, and kept copies of her books with him to the end of his life.

Like many other European intellectuals, Clovis was forced by the failure of the 1848 revolutions to look to the new world. There was no future for a liberal journalist in the

France of Louis Napoléon. No doubt impressed by his wife's South American connections, he decided to emigrate to Peru and start a newspaper there. Unfortunately, although aged only 35, he died of a heart attack on the long voyage round Cape Horn, and was buried in Patagonia. With her two babies, his young widow had no choice but to complete the voyage.

On arrival in Lima, Aline was well received by her Spanish grandfather's younger brother, Don Pio de Tristan Moscoso. His position in Peruvian society is indicated by the fact that, only a few months after Aline's arrival, Don Pio's son-in-law, Echenique, became President of Peru. Aline and her two young children consequently found themselves in a tropical paradise where every material need was met and every sense was indulged.

'I have a remarkable visual memory, and I remember that period, our house and a whole lot of events', Gauguin said later. He was an eighteen-month-old baby when he arrived in Lima, a six-year-old-boy when he left, and one can imagine the indelible impressions of Peru that haunted him all his life. The small child grew up bathed in the dry heat and the brilliant sunlight, surrounded by the shapes and scents of an exotic vegetation, and no doubt endlessly cherished by his colourful relatives and their many servants. Aline and her two children were looked after by a Negro nursemaid and a Chinese manservant; and the racial diversity of Peru was matched by a rich extravagance of dress and by the brightly painted buildings everywhere in the city.

Suddenly for the child Gauguin this world disappeared, and he was flung into the grey, miserable, money-scraping existence of provincial France. He could hardly have appreciated the sequence of events – a civil war in Peru which resulted in Don Pio's family losing political power, Aline's return to France anticipating grandfather Gauguin's death, life with Clovis's bachelor brother in Orléans, a small legacy from the Gauguins, and a large annuity from Don Pio, which his family prevented Aline from ever receiving. Eventually she established herself as a dressmaker in Paris, leaving Paul at boarding school in Orléans.

It is not surprising that his one ambition was to escape, and find again that lost paradise of childhood. Gauguin had a strong practical streak, and the obvious solution was to go to sea as soon as he was old enough. So, in December 1865, the three-master *Luzitano* left Le Havre for Rio, with the 17-year-old Paul on board. For two years with the merchant marine, and a further three with the French navy, Gauguin sailed the world, crossing the Pacific, patrolling the Atlantic, seeing naval action in the Franco-Prussian war. He did not in fact return to Peru: perhaps the occasion never arrived, perhaps he would not have taken it even if it had.

During his longest voyage away, Gauguin's mother died. Though only 41, her health had been declining, and in her last years she had lived in semi-retirement in Saint Cloud. A wealthy banker neighbour, Gustave Arosa and his wife, had taken an interest in Aline and her children, and Arosa was named their legal guardian in her will. It was an excellent choice. When Paul in 1871 decided that the rootless, wandering life of the sailor was after all not for him, Arosa found him an opening as a broker's agent in the Paris stock exchange.

Gauguin settled down to bourgeois existence in Paris very quickly. In November 1873 he married Mette Gad, a young Danish governess whom he had met not long before. In 1874 the first of their five children was born. Gauguin was only a tolerably successful business man, but in 1880 the young couple were able to move to a large, comfortable suburban house in Vaugirard with a garden for the children and a studio for Paul to paint in.

For already Paul's 'hobby' was beginning to take up more and more of his time and his energies. It seems probable that he began painting in the summer of 1873, when his fiancée was at home in Denmark preparing for the wedding. Mette claimed that she did not know of her husband's painting activities when she married him and there is no reason to disbelieve her. The introduction to art, like the introduction to Mette, came through Gustave Arosa. He was an enthusiast, with an excellent private collection of modern paintings – many works by Delacroix, some Corots, Courbets, Jongkinds,

Pissarros, as well as pieces of oriental and exotic pottery. Arosa's daughter Marguerite was a Sunday painter, and it was probably she who introduced Paul to brushes and canvas, perhaps to pass the time while Mette was away.

Admittedly Gauguin had no formal training and attended only a few classes at art college, but it is worth emphasizing that he started painting when just 25, that he devoted a great deal of time to it, and that he benefited from the particularly valuable kind of instruction which ownership of works of art can bring. Emulating his guardian, he had begun to collect as well as paint, buying the works which he needed to study to further his own artistic career. At first he chose straightforward naturalistic landscapes by Jongkind and Pissarro, then bought representative examples of others associated with the revolutionary impressionist group – Manet, Monet, Renoir, Degas, and, most difficult but most rewarding of all, Cézanne. Most of Gauguin's picture-buying was done in 1879, a year when spare cash was easily available. This patronage in turn made it easier for Gauguin to show his own paintings in the exhibitions of the impressionists.

The major influence on Gauguin in this early phase of his career was certainly that of Camille Pissarro, whose advice and encouragement meant much to Gauguin, as it did to Cézanne and to Van Gogh.

Pissarro was the key figure behind the scenes in the crisis years of 1882 and 1883 when Gauguin lost his job and became a full-time painter. The exact course of events which led to this decision cannot now be reconstructed. 1882 was a year of financial crisis in France, when bankruptcies abounded, and perhaps business was so bad that Gauguin optimistically thought he could earn a better living by selling his own pictures. He had good reason for feeling that painting was now too important to be only a part-time activity – had not Huysmans singled out his nude study for praise at the 1881 impressionist exhibition? Had he not now won the support of Degas as well as of Pissarro? – Degas whose influence is so pronounced in the ambitious figure pictures that Gauguin did in 1881 (plate 2)?

Gauguin's adroit practice of furthering his own artistic progress by taking what he needed from established contemporaries inevitably led to personal difficulties. In November 1883 he abandoned Paris as being too expensive for a full-time artist, and moved to Rouen. He wanted to be near Pissarro, with whom he had grown accustomed to working in summer vacations; but the many landscapes of 1884 show Gauguin more interested in Cézanne's work than in Pissarro's, and it must have saddened Pissarro to see his gifted pupil drifting away. Cézanne for his part was (and always remained) deeply suspicious of Gauguin, whom he suspected of stealing his ideas. Gauguin was passing through that natural stage in any major artist's development when he absorbs what is going on around him before making the decisive leap forward himself.

One can argue I think that Gauguin's ideas about what art should be were crystallizing faster than his ability to express them in paint on canvas. After a year in Rouen marked by intense activity and increasing financial problems, Gauguin left to join his wife in Copenhagen. Mette had sensibly decided that it was hopeless to expect her husband to support her and the five children by sales of paintings; the only solution was to return to her family in Denmark, where at least she could work as translator and French teacher. Gauguin followed, and was evidently thoroughly humiliated. In his isolation, he turned for the first time to paint himself (plate 1). Gauguin also had time to think, and in a letter to his friend and former colleague Schuffenecker tried to find words to describe his new ideas. The appeal of painting, he says, must be total, must work through all the senses. A naturalistic approach, he implies, is not enough; colours, lines, repetition of shapes can in themselves communicate emotions to the beholder.

It was not immediately obvious to Gauguin how all this could be put into practice. On his return to France without Mette, in the summer of 1885, he continued to work hard, but was restless, moving from place to place. Constantly in financial difficulties, he briefly visited London as a courier for Spanish revolutionary friends. A curious consequence of this trip may be the *Still Life with Horse's Head* (plate 4), which offers a programmatic union of Greek and Japanese in its juxtaposition of the horse's head from the Elgin marbles against the Japanese hand puppet and fans.

5

Gauguin seems to have returned from Denmark determined to play the part of an artist with a message. The leadership of the avant-garde in 1885 was held decisively by Seurat, whose pseudo-scientific neo-impressionism was quickly attracting disciples – including Signac and the now middle-aged Pissarro. Gauguin made some tentative experiments in this direction – the *Still Life with Horse's Head* is one – and became friendly with Signac. He could hardly have failed to be involved in the discussions around Seurat's *La Grande Jatte*, which was shown at the eighth and last impressionist exhibition in May 1886.

There was no doubt a certain deep-rooted tension in the quarrel with Seurat that broke out at this moment. Gauguin said that he had Signac's permission to use his Paris studio for the summer: but Signac had left the key with Seurat, who claimed to know nothing about the offer and would not take Gauguin's word. Perhaps on an impulse after this rejection, Gauguin in June 1886 left Paris for Pont Aven in Brittany.

It was not however a sudden decision: Gauguin had been thinking of going to Brittany for at least a year. It was the first decisive step towards the primitive environment that he had come to feel was necessary if his art was to develop.

Gauguin stayed until November, painting better than before, but not yet having found himself as an artist. The subject matter was right, but not the treatment. The debts to the older impressionists are still strong in such paintings as *The Dance of the Four Breton Girls* (plate 7) and *The Bathers* (plate 8). Degas in particular is the major influence here; but in some of the landscapes it is Monet one thinks of; and in other works, like the *Still Life with the Profile of Laval* (plate 5), it is Cézanne. Gauguin was endlessly talking about finding a synthesis, but somehow it eluded him. Though he had a natural authority among the other painters at Pont Aven, he was not yet flamboyant or over-confident. The Scots painter, A. S. Hartrick, gives us an excellent description of Gauguin's physical appearance at this time:

> 'Tall, dark-haired and swarthy of skin, heavy of eyelid and with handsome features, all combined with a powerful figure. . . . He dressed like a Breton fisherman in a blue jersey and wore a beret jauntily at the side of his head. His general appearance, walk and all, was rather that of a well-to-do Biscayan skipper of a coasting schooner; nothing could be further from madness or decadence. In manner he was self-contained and confident, silent and almost dour, though he could unbend and be quite charming when he liked.'

Gauguin needed this taciturn self-containment, for the next months of his life were hard indeed. He spent the winter in Paris, painting little but making extraordinarily inventive ceramics in the workshop of the potter, Chaplet. He was ill in hospital for a month, and now began to dream of leaving inhospitable France for a warmer climate. In April 1887 he embarked for Panama, where his sister's husband was working – for she, perhaps subject to the same romantic Peruvian dream that affected her brother, had married a South American business man. But Gauguin's idea of an easy life in the tropics had to meet the reality of poverty, illness and neglect; and even the comparative haven of the French island of Martinique soon became unbearable. Gauguin had to work his passage back to France as a deck-hand, bringing with him a dozen pictures (among them plate 9) whose brighter colours and tapestry-like design show the first clear signs of a break with impressionism.

Gauguin had little inclination now to stay in Paris, and in February 1888 left for Brittany again. Thus began the most decisive, most prolific, two-year period of his entire career. He was beginning to feel closer to that long sought synthesis that seemed to be the secret of painting. For the moment he was in the right surroundings. He told Schuffenecker: 'You're a Parisian, but give me the country. I love Brittany. I find a wildness and a primitiveness there. When my wooden shoes ring out on its granite soil, I hear the muffled, dull and powerful note I am looking for in my painting.'

Gauguin was finding out more about himself. Before leaving Paris he had written to Mette: 'You must remember that there are two natures in me: the Indian, and the sensitive man. The sensitive man has now disappeared, letting the Indian go ahead strong and straight.'

At first the 'Indian savage' was too ill to paint, and the weather was bad, but when spring came he began to work in earnest, finishing two and even three pictures a week. But they were not so very different from what he had done two years before, and it was not until Émile Bernard arrived early in August with some new paintings that Gauguin suddenly realized he could go much further in the direction he was already moving.

'Little Bernard', as Gauguin called him, was only twenty, but he was a brilliant and precocious talent. He had just invented a new manner of painting that was promptly labelled *cloissonism*: this had given Bernard a certain standing in the Parisian avant-garde. Like many others, he was looking for a visual equivalent of the symbolist poetry and prose that was strongly emerging in reaction against naturalism. His idea was to express only the essence of any subject, with the simplest of means – a few thick, black lines, dividing flat, bright colours.

Gauguin saw the point at once. On 14th August 1888, he wrote to Schuffenecker: 'A word of advice. Don't paint too much after nature. Art is an abstraction. Extract it from nature by dreaming in front of it, and think more of the creation which will result.'

Responding to Bernard's stimulus, Gauguin immediately went far beyond his young friend's ideas – and this is the essential of their relationship. Bernard painted *Breton Women in the Meadow*, showing peasants dressed for the Pardon of Pont Aven, and introducing two ladies in city costume. Gauguin liked this picture so much, that he made an exchange with Bernard; and he took it with him to Arles to show Vincent Van Gogh. But he had seen at once that the naturalistic subject matter was inadequate in itself, and must somehow be transcended. He wanted to 'invoke beautiful thoughts with form and colour', as he told Schuffenecker. The result was the *Vision after the Sermon* (plate 10), Gauguin's first unquestioned masterpiece, and the turning point of his entire oeuvre.

Instead of simply painting Breton women, Gauguin tries to express in paint a *quality* that he admires – the simple faith that allows these peasant folk, when leaving church after a particularly vivid sermon, to have a vision of what has been described to them. He disposes of the women round two sides of his composition, rather as Bernard does, but he paints the green field red, and places on it the struggling figures of Jacob and the Angel, freely adapted from a Hokusai print of wrestlers, that he either owned or had copied. The idea of painting a religious subject probably came from Van Gogh, who in correspondence with Gauguin said that he had been trying unsuccessfully to paint a *Christ in the Garden of Olives*.

Gauguin wanted to give the picture to a local church. That at Pont Aven was modern, so with his friends he carried the *Vision after the Sermon* across the fields to the nearby village of Nizon. Among the church's old stone piers and crude carved sculptures of saints the painting would be at home. He wrote in blue letters on the white frame: 'Gift of Tristan Moscoso'. It was a tribute from the Peruvian savage to primitive Brittany – but the curé, fearing a hoax, would not accept the gift, so the picture was removed.

The idea of remaining in Brittany for the cold, damp, winter months was unattractive, and in October Gauguin accepted the pressing invitation from Vincent Van Gogh to join him in Arles. He did so reluctantly, but out of an obligation to Vincent's brother, Theo, who was the first art dealer to give Gauguin the backing and support he needed. The story of the ten tumultuous weeks in Arles is well enough known, and there is every reason to feel that a temperamental incompatibility between the two men made the rupture inevitable. 'Vincent likes my paintings very much', Gauguin told Bernard, 'but when I do them he always finds faults. He is a romantic, but I am rather drawn towards the primitive.'

It is very clear – and psychologically convincing – that Gauguin saw himself as the master, and that Vincent gladly accepted the role of pupil. With all the fervour of the newly converted, Gauguin now knew what ought to be done. Don't paint from nature. Art is an abstraction. One must work from memory. All were precepts calculated to reduce Vincent to despair. But Gauguin took Vincent's subjects, such as the *Night Café*, and showed him how they should be painted (plate 14). Vincent had been working in the public garden at Arles. Let us meditate on this subject, one imagines Gauguin saying, what does it suggest to you? I am reminded of the women of Brittany (plate 11), but don't you think of your mother and sister, as they used to walk in the garden of your father's house at Etten before you left Holland? You must introduce them into your picture – and this Vincent dutifully did in his painting, *Women in the Garden* (*Souvenir of Etten*).

Gauguin thought that his most successful picture at Arles was the one in which he painted Breton women in an Arles vineyard – 'so much the worse for accuracy'. He called it *Human Anguish* (plate 15), and the title is an indication of what he wanted art to express.

Vincent, for his part, couldn't follow where Gauguin led. 'I can't work from memory,' we find him repeatedly telling his brother, 'I can't work without a model.' Weeks later, when his dream of the atelier in the South had collapsed, Vincent was to write to Émile Bernard: 'When Gauguin was in Arles, as you know I once or twice allowed myself to be led to abstractions. At the time, this road to the abstract seemed to me a charming track. But it's an enchanted land, my dear friend, and soon one finds oneself up against an insurmountable wall.'

An 'enchanted land' however was just what Gauguin sought in his own art.

Gauguin wasn't able to paint much in Paris. He made pots, and lithographs on zinc of earlier subjects. It was the year of the Universal Exhibition of 1889: the Eiffel Tower was being erected, and in artistic circles there was much discussion of the art shows. Excluded from the official exhibition, Gauguin and his friends got permission to hang their pictures in the Café des Arts. They called themselves the *Impressionist and Synthetist Group*. Their work made little impact on the public: but among the painters it confirmed Gauguin's position at the head of a new movement, now challenging the avant-garde primacy of Seurat's neo-impressionism.

Gauguin was more interested in the Universal Exhibition itself, and especially the colonial section, with its reconstructions of the temple of Angkor-Wat and of a Javanese village, complete with native huts and dancing girls. He was collecting photographs of Buddhist and especially of Cambodian art: at this time he was thinking of going to Tonkin in French Indo-China, and had begun to negotiate with the French Colonial Office. This took time, and while waiting Gauguin decided to go back to Brittany.

He spent most of the summer at Pont Aven, but the village was now becoming too crowded, too civilized for his tastes. In October Gauguin moved with his disciples and supporters, Meyer de Haan and Paul Sérusier, to the remote hamlet of Le Pouldu, where they settled at the inn of Marie Henry. She became Meyer de Haan's mistress, and complaisantly allowed the painters to decorate the living room as they wished. On the doors of a wooden cupboard, Gauguin painted caricature portraits of Meyer de Haan and of himself (plate 18). Above the *Caribbean Woman* (plate 19) on the entrance doorway, he made another version of *Bonjour M. Gauguin*. These are frankly decorative pictures, and Gauguin is free of naturalistic constraints: he adopts highly stylized forms, simplified colours and he deliberately keeps the surfaces very flat.

Bonjour M. Gauguin (plate 17) was an explicit homage to Courbet, whose painting *Bonjour M. Courbet* Gauguin had seen when he visited Montpellier with Van Gogh. It is sometimes presumed that Gauguin is mocking Courbet's pretensions, but there is no evidence whatsoever for believing this. On the contrary, it would appear that Gauguin appreciated that Courbet's placing of himself at the centre of his painting was not simply arrogant egotism but artistic necessity. It represented a basic shift in the nature of nineteenth century painting, as the artist gradually removed subject matter from a public domain to a private one.

Following Courbet's example, Gauguin proceeds to make it clear that, whatever he is ostensibly painting, his art is firmly centred on himself. In the caricature self portrait (plate 18) he gives himself a halo, but the apples and serpent indicate that this is Gauguin as Lucifer, the devil himself. Not content with a fashionable Satanism, Gauguin also presents himself as Christ. The triptych of religious paintings executed in the autumn of 1889 – the *Agony in the Garden*, the *Crucifixion* and the *Deposition* – use the symbolic Christian events, but to entirely personal ends. Gauguin was not a Christian, and, unlike his friend Bernard, he had no desire to revive religious painting. If he had painted the *Vision after the Sermon*, it was because he admired the simple faith of the Breton women, so strong that it could inspire visions. With both the *Crucifixion*, or *Yellow Christ* (plate 20) and the *Deposition*, or *Green Christ* (plate 21) Gauguin takes a local carving – the polychrome wooden crucifix from Trémalo, and the stone Calvary of Nizon – and reinterprets it against a local landscape background – Pont Aven for the *Crucifixion*, Le Pouldu for the *Deposition*. In the *Crucifixion* appear the Breton women from the *Vision after the Sermon*, as if to stress the connection with the earlier painting.

Gauguin gave the young critic Albert Aurier some cryptic notes about the *Green Christ*, which seem to suggest that he could appreciate what religious belief meant for the Breton, and yet could see no way in which he could share it. This surely is the meaning of *Bonjour M. Gauguin*, where the gate bars the heavily-shrouded painter from any real contact with the Breton peasant. Gauguin's isolation is dramatically emphasized by the storm clouds in the sky: he appears as a symbol of the loneliness and suffering that he had come to feel was the lot of the dedicated artist. It is not surprising that in the three religious paintings, Gauguin gradually edges towards the identification of himself with Christ. In the *Agony in the Garden*, or *Christ in the Garden of Olives* (plate 16), probably the last of the three to be painted, the features of Christ are clearly Gauguin's own: there exists also a self portrait which juxtaposes Gauguin's head with that of the Christ in the *Crucifixion*, and another later *Self Portrait*, which Gauguin inscribed 'Près de Golgotha'.

In such works, Gauguin does not seem to have been deliberately blasphemous. His own beliefs were profoundly influenced by the ideas of Schopenhauer, whose philosophy was popular in advanced intellectual circles in France at the time. There is no evidence that Gauguin actually read the work of the German philosopher, but he had come to share his pessimism and his preference for Buddhism over Christianity. He was also inclined to believe in the power of the will as the only way in which the nothingness of existence can be transcended, and to share Schopenhauer's conviction that the very exercise of the will is evil. A small portrait of Meyer de Haan painted late in 1889 has *Nirvana* written on it, as if to indicate the common aspiration of the two painters.

In a few words it is impossible to do justice to the complexity of Gauguin's thinking. That thinking is in any case expressed primarily through the medium of the painting and the sculpture, and lengthy analysis of each succeeding work of art would be necessary. Leaving naturalism behind, Gauguin now began to experiment with type-figures, which reappear from painting to painting, carrying with them a symbolic content. The seated nude woman with hands to her face in the background of *Nirvana* for example reappears in contemporary paintings as a Breton Eve, and again later in Gauguin's last testament, *Where do we come from? What are we? Where are we going?* (plates 44 and 45). One cannot interpret such type-figures in precise verbal terms, and this is an important characteristic of Gauguin's symbolism: there must always remain that vestigial sense of poetry, of mystery, of something too near the heart of things to be easily explicable.

Gauguin's problem in 1889–90 was to find the kind of subject that could carry the message of his painting. He had quickly exhausted the possibilities of Christian iconography, and though he concurrently painted a long series of Breton subjects, these were not altogether successful. *The Seaweed Harvesters* (plate 23) is the largest canvas of this period, yet it remains comparatively unknown; the *Breton Girls by the Sea* (plate 22) seems to hint at a significance greater than the ostensible subject, but without altogether convincing us. If we compare it with the *Loss of Virginity* (plate 25) we can appreciate what it was that Gauguin wanted to express.

A young girl lies naked in a landscape: her feet are crossed, like those of the Yellow Christ; one hand holds a flower, the other rests on the fox. He sits on her shoulder, with a paw on her heart, and is presumably the very same animal who had appeared in the carved relief *Be Loving*, when Gauguin described him as the Indian symbol of perversity. Here he seems to represent lubricity and sexual desire as well. Behind the girl is a line of flame-like foliage that isolates her, like a Brunnhilde awaiting Siegfried on the rocky mountain. In the distance, a Breton landscape with a procession of figures and on the horizon the sea. The title, *Loss of Virginity*, makes the meaning of the picture obvious – too obvious perhaps, because the painting is exceptional in Gauguin's oeuvre for the explicit nature of its symbolism. It might have been a demonstration piece: for the *Loss of Virginity* was probably completed in Paris in the last months of 1890, when Gauguin's contacts with symbolist literary figures were at their closest. Verlaine, Moréas, Morice, Barrès, Mallarmé became his friends, and Gauguin was now regarded in advanced circles as the outstanding painter of his generation. Public success, and a life free from material cares, were certainly within his grasp: the dream of a reconciliation with his wife and children could well have become a reality. Yet Gauguin wilfully rejected this because of the daemon that now drove him, in April 1891, to leave France for Tahiti.

Gauguin had been dreaming of going back to the tropics ever since his return from Martinique. As we have seen, after visiting the 1889 Exhibition he thought of going as a settler to Tonkin in French Indo-China. As he told Émile Bernard in June 1890: 'The whole Orient, great thoughts written in letters of gold on all the art – that is certainly worth study, and I'm sure I shall acquire new strength there. The West is rotten at this moment, and any young Hercules can, like Antaeus, find new strength by setting foot on that soil. You'd come back, a year or two later, sound and strong.'

At this moment Bernard read Pierre Loti's semi-autobiographical novel, *The Marriage of Loti*, first published under the Tahitian title *Rarahu* in 1880. Loti was a former naval officer, of the same age as Gauguin, who knew and admired his novels – *Icelandic Fishermen* of 1886, for example, which inspired Van Gogh's *Berceuse* paintings. Bernard sent *The Marriage of Loti* to Gauguin, and with it the official handbook to the French colonies, which had an enthusiastic essay on Tahiti. Gauguin hesitated no longer: it was to Tahiti that he would go. He succeeded in getting official permission to travel as an artist on an unpaid mission. This gave him status and certain financial advantages, although the verbal promise of purchase of pictures on his return was never kept.

Just before leaving, Gauguin paid a short visit to Copenhagen to see his wife and children. He had still not abandoned the idea of a reconciliation, although, apart from his 17-year-old daughter, Aline, he now found his family strangely alien to him. But Charles Morice records that Gauguin broke down on returning from Denmark, when he tearfully confessed to having sacrificed his family to his ideas.

Gauguin sailed from Marseilles on 1st April 1891, and arrived at Papeete, the capital of Tahiti, on 9th June. Three days later, hours before Gauguin's appointment to meet him, Pomare V, the last king of Tahiti, died. It was a bad augury. Gauguin was soon to realize that he had come to a down-at-heel French colony, and not to an island paradise untouched by Western civilization. He was in fact over a hundred years too late. Since the island's discovery by the West in 1767, the native population had fallen catastrophically from an estimated 150,000 to about 8,000, and virtually nothing now remained of the traditional religion, mythology and art.

After a few months Gauguin moved out of the unattractive little capital to the village of Mataiea on the beautiful south coast of the island, about eighty miles away. He had got to know the Francophile local chief, Tetuanui, and this seemed to offer a way of at least coming closer to native life. But Gauguin had no illusions about Tahiti: very soon after his arrival he was already seeking an appointment in the Marquesas Islands, another French possession.

Gauguin's attempts to move away from Tahiti into a more primitive environment were frustrated by the Governor, Lacascade, who saw in him a potential trouble maker. Bouts of illness, resulting from the syphilis that was eventually to kill him, and constant financial difficulties, were troubling Gauguin, and by June 1892 he was asking for repatriation to France. This was agreed in November, but Lacascade regretted that no funds for a passage were then available, and Gauguin had to wait until 14th June 1893 before he could leave. His first stay in Tahiti had lasted almost exactly two years.

Despite all the disappointments and discouragements, it was, after a slow beginning, a most rich and prolific time for his painting. Gauguin completed about eighty pictures, thirty of them by any reckoning masterpieces, and this is as many as he was to produce in the remaining ten years of his life. At first he was accustoming himself to the new surroundings, and in subject matter the pictures are a continuation of the kind of work he had been doing in Brittany – some landscapes, but mostly pictures of the local people at work and at play. For three or four months after settling in Mataiea in October 1891, Gauguin seems to have been completely happy, and this is reflected in his work. At Christmas he painted the idyllic *Ia Orana Maria* (plate 32) – the title is the first part of the Tahitian version of the Ave Maria – and the picture shows an angel with yellow wings pointing out to two Tahitian women the figures of Mary and Jesus. They are as Tahitians, just as the crucified Christ and the mourning women had been seen depicted as Bretons. *Ia Orana Maria* is the direct successor to the earlier religious paintings, and the changed mood reflects Gauguin's new-found and short-lived happiness in Tahiti.

Other Tahitian pictures of 1891–2 can be closely linked with earlier work. *Reverie* (plate 29) evokes a distinct mood, as does the *Loss of Virginity*; *Ta Matete* (plate 33) is a painting of prostitutes waiting for customers, like the Arles *Night Café* (plate 14). One can also compare *When will you marry?* (plate 30) to the *Breton Girls by the Sea* (plate 22); or the *Woman with a Flower* (plate 26) – the first of Gauguin's Tahitian paintings to be exhibited in Paris – to earlier portrait studies. But there is also a new strangeness about the paintings. Probably none were done direct from nature: Gauguin continued to work from memory in his studio, and certain elements and stock figures reappear from picture to picture. He was also introducing frankly exotic references into his compositions. As he later told de Monfried: 'Have always before you the Persians, the *Cambodians*, and a little of the Egyptians. The great error is the Greek, however beautiful it may be.' This explains the conscious and deliberate borrowings from Khmer art, for example, in the poses of the two Tahitian women in *Ia Orana Maria* which are taken directly from a photograph Gauguin had of part of the frieze of the Javanese temple of Borobudur; also the use of Egyptian reliefs, allegedly seen in the British Museum, for the women on the bench in *Ta Matete*.

No doubt Gauguin would have also introduced motifs from Tahitian art, had there been anything to introduce. All that was left locally were the traditional colours and patterns of the *pareos* – the loose-fitting dresses worn by the women. Gauguin liked them, because they accorded well with the tendency of his more considered pictures at this time to be very flat and abstract in conception – for example, *Near the Sea* (plates 35 and 36) and the large *Pastorales Tahitiennes* (plate 34). Gauguin was particularly pleased with the latter, a larger version of the painting now in the Louvre which he called *Joyeusetés* (fun, or amusement). He was beginning to feel able to express his vision of Tahitian existence in an artistically convincing way.

That it was a vision of existence and not a copy of the real thing should always be borne in mind. For Gauguin was now reconstructing in his own paintings the perfect life which he had failed to find in reality. On a visit to Papeete in March 1892 he had been lent a book about Tahiti before the Europeans had arrived which, though full of false interpretations, was nevertheless to stimulate his imagination and enrich his painting. This was J.–A. Moerenhout's *Voyage aux îles du grand océan*, published in 1837, when the disintegration of Tahitian society was already well under way.

Moerenhout's book was full of Tahitian legend and history, and Gauguin was fascinated by the accounts of the long vanished Arioi, a priestly élite whose communion services were sexual as well as religious. He painted the Arioi's legendary beauty, Vairaumati; and he painted the moon goddess Hina (plate 39), the only Tahitian female divinity, and the ancestral mother of the gods and the human race. As the Tahitians never made any idols, Gauguin had to invent one, mixing hints of Buddha, Pharaoh and Easter Island statue to make a satisfactory image.

Recent research, by Bengt Danielsson in particular, has given us a much clearer idea of the relationship between the actuality of Gauguin's Tahitian existence, and the pictures that he painted. This can only make us respect still more Gauguin's courage and his imagination. His own account of his life, *Noa-Noa*, blends fact with fiction, but there is no reason to expect veracity from an artist whose whole existence was now being lived out on the edge of dream. There was no other way of surviving the illness, the poverty, the loneliness, the total lack of understanding, that Gauguin had to face.

Not that Gauguin did not also have his moments of happiness and tranquillity, as the paintings themselves show. Cruelty and ugliness is banished from them, though fear and a sense of awe and mystery are sometimes present. When he took a native bride in the thirteen-year-old Teha'amana (the Tehura of *Noa-Noa*), Gauguin found a new depth of inspiration. He knew that *Manao Tupapau* (plate 31) was a masterpiece, and often wrote about it. The initial inspiration was Gauguin's return home one night to find Teha'amana lying face down on her bed, gripped with terror at the darkness. She seemed to Gauguin both very beautiful, but also very foreign, looking at him as if he were the *tupapau* – the demon that lies in wait during sleepless nights. Gauguin began to think about man's fear of darkness and of death – and this is what his picture is about. He wrote of the picture: 'Let us sum it up. Musical part: undulating horizontal lines; blue and orange harmonies, linked with yellows and purples (their derivatives) and lit by greenish sparks. Literary part: the spirit of a living soul united with the spirit of the dead. Night and Day.'

Thus the painter's idea is conveyed directly through abstract means as well as by literary connotations. This is pictorial symbolism of a very high order.

Gauguin arrived back in Paris on 1st September 1893: as might have been expected at this time of year, all his friends were still out of town. It was an inauspicious beginning, and Gauguin had now lived too long in Tahiti to feel at home in what was then the most civilized city in the world. He had lost contact with people, and could never recapture that feeling of being at the hub of all advanced creative activity which had been his in 1890–91. In any case the mood of Paris had changed: a reaction against experiment in the arts was setting in, and was to last for a decade. The anarchist bomb attacks, the Panama scandal, the Dreyfus case were all indicative of a general atmosphere of unease.

No doubt through the faithful Degas's good offices, Gauguin had an opportunity of showing forty-four of the best Tahitian pictures at the prestigious gallery of Durand-Ruel. Public reaction was generally antipathetic: there were some lukewarm reviews, and a few sales, mostly to old friends. Gauguin was disappointed: nobody seemed to understand what he was getting at. He was too dejected to do much painting, and welcomed Charles Morice's suggestion that they should collaborate on a book about Tahiti – this was to be entitled *Noa-Noa*, the Fragrant Isle. They worked together over Gauguin's notes, Morice preparing a draft text and Gauguin making woodcuts to illustrate it.

In the summer of 1894 Gauguin returned to Pont Aven, but the spirit of the place that had once meant so much now eluded him. There is a curiously detached quality about the *Drame au Village* (Chicago, Art Institute), and this is perhaps confirmed by the fact that nobody is quite certain whether it was in fact painted during this summer. In the foreground is that same seated woman with hands to her face who first appeared in *Human Anguish* (plate 15): we have already noticed her nude counterpart in *Nirvana* and *Where do we come from?* . . . (see plates 44–5). And the problems of human communication that the *Drame au Village* seems to raise were now becoming increasingly real for Gauguin. Contemporaries speak of him as being aloof, taciturn, arrogantly self-confident – rather different from the convivial and gregarious artist of earlier years. Experience of living virtually alone for long periods now made Gauguin turn in on himself, hardening his heart against human feelings. Relations with Mette were worsening; and his former mistress Juliette Huet broke with Gauguin completely because of his infatuation with the thirteen-year-old Annah, the so-called Javanese – she was in fact half Indian and half Malay. When he painted Annah, however (plate 40), Gauguin wrote on the picture a Tahitian sentence meaning 'The child-woman Judith is not yet breached' – a scabrous reference to another nymphet, the Swedish twelve-year-old Judith Erikson-Molard, whose company Gauguin liked to keep.

The details of Gauguin's life at this time have a sordid, distasteful quality, as if to prove the rotten, degenerate nature of life in the West. That he was suffering increasingly from the widespread effects of syphilis is now clear to us: whether Gauguin appreciated this is less evident. He was anxious to be off again: he wrote in September 1894 to Judith's stepfather, William Molard: 'I have taken the irrevocable decision . . . Nothing will stop me going, and it will be for good. How stupid an existence European life is.' Again there was an auction sale of paintings to raise money, Gauguin using as preface Strindberg's letter declining the invitation to write it. The sale in February 1895 was disappointing but not disastrous. Gauguin was ready to go. It was only the need for more hospital treatment that made him postpone his departure from Paris until the end of June.

Gauguin arrived at Papeete on 8th September 1895, but, this time, he had no intention of staying on Tahiti: he was going to go on directly to Dominique in the Marquesas. We do not know why he changed his plans; it was probably because his health was deteriorating, and he knew he could only get hospital treatment if he stayed within reach of Papeete. He decided to have a native house built at Punaauia, on the coast about twenty miles south of the capital, and this remained his home until he finally left Tahiti in 1901. Teha'amana was summoned, but, frightened by Gauguin's running sores, she refused to stay with him. Another 14-year-old, Pahura, took her place.

Gauguin's life was a mixture of tranquillity and relative contentment, when the painting went well, and appalling suffering, both mental and physical, when he could do nothing at all. The flat, bright colours of 1892–4 give way to a grave and sonorous tonality. *Nevermore* (plate 41) is characteristic. Gauguin wrote of it to his friend and loyal correspondent, Daniel de Monfried:

'I wanted to suggest with a simple nude a certain barbarian luxury of times past. The whole is suffused in colours which are deliberately sombre and sad. It is neither silk, nor velvet, nor batiste, nor gold which makes this luxury, but simply matter which has been enriched by the artist's hand. No nonsense – man's imagination alone has enriched the dwelling with his fantasy.

'As a title, *Nevermore* (in English): not the raven of Edgar Poe, but the bird of the devil that is keeping watch. It's badly painted (I'm so on edge and can only work in bouts), but no matter, I think it's a good picture.'

The letter was written on 14th February 1897; as the year went on disaster followed disaster. Gauguin's landlord dies, and he has to move house. He learns of the death from pneumonia of his favourite child, Aline, and this leads to the final rupture with Mette. He is penniless, unable to walk because his foot is so painful, unable to paint because of conjunctivitis. In August he writes to Molard: 'Since my childhood, misfortune has dogged me. Never a chance, never any happiness. Everything always against me, and I cry out: Oh God, if you exist, I accuse you of injustice, of malice. Yes, on hearing of poor Aline's death, I doubted everything, I laughed in defiance. What use is virtue, hard work, courage, intelligence? Only crime is logical and makes any sense.' In September he is in despair. 'I can see nothing except Death which delivers us from everything.' In October a succession of heart attacks leads Gauguin to talk of suicide. For six months he has painted nothing: now he makes a final heroic effort. 'I wanted before dying to paint a big picture which I had in my head', he told de Monfried, 'and for a month I worked night and day in an unheard-of fever'.

The result was Gauguin's largest and most ambitious picture, on which he wrote the words: *Where do we come from? What are we? Where are we going?* (plates 44 and 45). Thus it is intended as a philosophic statement about the meaning of life, though before trying to explain it we do well to heed Gauguin's own warning: 'My dream is intangible, it implies no allegory. To quote Mallarmé: "a musical poem, it needs no libretto". As it is above the material, the essence of a work lies precisely in "what is not expressed" . . .'

Yet Gauguin also wrote more explicitly about the painting, and his reticence cannot conceal its obvious lesson. It was a dream, he said, painted out of his head – and it is peopled with figures who have appeared in many earlier pictures. It is full of animals, children and child-like 'savages', who live out their lives in a garden of Eden. Yet it is no innocent, virginal world, but one imbued with a latent eroticism. Every gesture, every symbol, almost every form proposes a sexual meaning; it is a dream of infantile sexuality that confronts us, as though Gauguin was here at last back in that warm, dimly-remembered, lost paradise of early childhood.

The central figure is a man plucking fruit from a tree, and we know what that implies. But it cannot be innocence that is lost; it is the thirst for knowledge, for awareness for anything beyond a crass acceptance of physical existence that marks the undoing of man. Many years before Gauguin had seen his destiny plainly when he wrote to Schuffenecker: 'According to legend, the Inca came straight from the sun, and I shall return there . . . Vincent sometimes calls me the man who came from far and will go far. I hope I shall be followed by all those good people who have loved and understood me. A better world is coming, where nature will follow its course; man will live in the sun, and know how to love.'

But by the time he had come to paint *Where do we come from? . . .*, Gauguin had lost his earlier optimism. Love has its dark side too: Eros is compounded with Thanatos, and the golden age is also an age when life is little more than bare survival from birth to death. All human endeavour he came to see as futile, as likely to result in evil as in good. 'Before us there is certainly only nothingness' – the words are Schopenhauer's but could equally well be Gauguin's. The only possible response was the private one proposed by the one man constantly in Gauguin's thoughts: the poet Mallarmé – one could create a work of art. And in *Where do we come from? . . .* Gauguin speaks as one who knows and has seen all: this is the final message that he wants to leave behind for perpetuity.

Gauguin's suicide attempt failed – he took too much arsenic, and instead of being poisoned was miserably sick. Gauguin accepted this last trick of fate, and didn't try again, but the final years of his life are a kind of coda to what has gone before. Dying of syphilis, he was living on borrowed time, and though he eventually got to the Marquesas and a little closer to the 'heart of savage of darkness' that he sought, it was too late to make any substantial difference to his life or to his art.

For long periods in the last five years – he died on 8th May 1903 – Gauguin did no painting at all. His time was fully taken up working as a draughtsman in the office of Public Works at Papeete, or as a journalist active in local politics. It is a destiny that inevitably reminds one of Rimbaud's life as a trader in Abyssinia – both men had taken art too far and suffered for it.

But unlike Rimbaud, Gauguin never completely abandoned his art: indeed 1902 is a comparatively prolific year, and the strange and vivid colours of the Marquesan paintings introduce a new note into his painting. *L'Appel* and *Contes Barbares* (plate 48) are among Gauguin's greatest paintings: there is a certain radiant tranquillity about them, as though Gauguin had reached an understanding of his fate.

Three years after Gauguin's death an enormous exhibition of his work opened at the Salon d'Automne in Paris. It was one of the most influential art exhibitions ever held, and directly from it much of the art of the twentieth century has sprung. In this respect Gauguin's only rival is Cézanne – a greater painter, as he would always have agreed – but Gauguin's influence has probably been more profound and wide-ranging.

For Gauguin transcends both the symbolism and the impressionism of the late nineteenth century. With him ends the pursuit of appearances, the obsession with the experience of perception that for so long had dominated European art. He rejected the painting of the impressionists because 'they seek around the eye and not at the mysterious centre of thought'.

14

So art turns inwards, away from appearances. Towards dream and the unconscious, towards an abstract art where colour and form alone convey the painting's meaning. To make this breakthrough somebody had to turn to the primitive as a means of liberating art from the great classical – Renaissance – naturalist tradition. Gauguin was not against this tradition – in certain respects his own painting embodies it – but he thought that it, like Western civilization as a whole, had come to an end. And he turned the private psychological necessity which provided the driving force for his whole career into a means of regenerating European art. Regression for the man meant primitivism for the painter.

In one of his last letters to de Monfried Gauguin wrote: 'You have known for a long time what I wanted to establish: *the right* to dare everything. My capacities . . . have not led to any great result, but at least the machine is in motion. The public owes me nothing, since my pictorial work is only *relatively* good, but the painters who, today, are profiting from this freedom, do owe me something.'

Gauguin was for once over-modest, but his clear-sighted honesty is appealing. As he had said in 1898 'the martyr is often necessary for a revolution. My work has little importance compared to its consequences: the freeing of painting from all restrictions.' After Gauguin, everything was possible.

Outline biography

1848 Born on 7 June, son of Aline and Clovis Gauguin, a political journalist.

1849 Clovis Gauguin has to flee Paris under the new government, and sets off with his family for Lima in Peru. He dies en route on 30 October.

1855 Madame Gauguin returns with her family to France, and settles at Orléans, where Paul is sent to school.

1864 Prepares to enter the École Navale, but instead, in 1865, joins the merchant navy and sails on board the *Luzitano*, plying between Rio de Janeiro and Le Havre.

1866 As a second lieutenant on board the *Chili*, he sails round the world.

1867 Death of Madame Gauguin.

1868 Transfers to the French Navy to do his military service, and sails on the imperial yacht *Jérôme-Napoléon* (later called *Desaix*).

1871 Leaves the navy, and, encouraged by his friend and guardian, Gustave Arosa, he becomes a stock-broking agent in the firm of Bertin.

1873 Summer: probably begins to paint, in the company of Arosa's daughter. 22 November: marries Mette Sophie Gad, a Danish governess working in Paris.

1874 31 August: his first son, Émile, is born.

1876 A landscape is accepted by the Salon. He begins to buy paintings.

1878 Becomes a friend of Pissarro, who encourages him to paint.

1879–82 Paintings shown at the exhibitions of the Impressionists.

1883 Stops work at the Bourse to devote himself to painting.

1884 With his family, leaves Paris to move to Rouen, and, in December, to Copenhagen.

1885 June: returns to Paris with his son Clovis. Brief visit to London and Dieppe, where he sees Degas.

1886 Probably begins to make ceramics; quarrels with Seurat; June–November in Pont-Aven, Brit-tany. Winter in Paris, where he meets Theo and Vincent van Gogh.

1887 April: leaves France for the Panama Canal. In June, moves to Martinique, but falls ill with dysentery and has to work his passage back to France in October.

1888 February: returns to Pont-Aven. In October, he goes to Arles, where he joins van Gogh; they quarrel on Christmas Eve, and Gauguin goes back to Paris.

1889 June: Gauguin and his friends hold an exhibition in the Café des Arts. He returns to Pont-Aven, moving later to the secluded village of Le Pouldu.

1890–1 Now recognized as a leading painter, and the representative of symbolism in painting. Close contact with symbolist poets, including Mallarmé, who presides over a farewell banquet on 23 March 1891. In May he arrives in Tahiti, and later settles at Mataiea with Teha'amana. He becomes seriously ill, and asks for repatriation.

1893 Returns to Paris, where he inherits a small legacy. He writes *Noa-Noa* with Charles Morice.

1895 Unable to settle happily in France, he decides to return to the Pacific. Holds a sale of his works, and embarks for Tahiti, settling in Punaauia.

1896 With Pahura.

1897 In April, he hears of the death of his daughter Aline, and is greatly upset. Paints his largest picture, *Where do we come from? . . .*

1898 January: attempted suicide. In May, takes post as a government draughtsman in Papeete. Begins to write in local newspapers.

1899 Stops painting for journalistic activities.

1901 Moves in November to Hiva-Oa in the Marquesas. Increasingly troubled by illness, he nevertheless begins painting again.

1903 Accused by the local authorities of trying to stir up local anarchy and sentenced to three months' imprisonment. He appeals, but dies on 8 May, at the age of 55. He is buried in Atuona.

1906 Large retrospective exhibition at *Salon d'Automne* in Paris.

List of plates

1. *Gauguin at his Easel.* 65 × 54 cm. 1885. Berne, Dr. Jacques Koerfer

2. *Interior of the Artist's Home in Paris, Rue Carcel.* 130 × 162 cm. 1881. Oslo, National Gallery

3. *The Snow, Rue Carcel.* 117 × 90 cm. 1883. Copenhagen, Madame Eva Kiaer

4. *Still Life with Horse's Head.* 49 × 38 cm. 1885. Paris, Private Collection

5. *Still Life with the Profile of Laval.* 46 × 38 cm. Mrs. Walter B. Ford II

6. *The Beach at Dieppe.* 71·5 × 71·5 cm. 1885. Copenhagen, Ny Carlsberg Glyptothek

7. *The Dance of the Four Breton Girls.* 72 × 91 cm. 1886. Munich, Bayerische Staatsgemäldesammlungen

8. *The Bathers.* 92 × 72 cm. 1887. Buenos Aires, Di Tella Collection

9. *Tropical Vegetation, Martinique.* 115·5 × 89 cm. 1887. Edinburgh, National Gallery of Scotland

10. *The Vision after the Sermon.* 74·4 × 93·1 cm. 1888. Edinburgh, National Gallery of Scotland

11. *In the Garden at Arles.* 73 × 91·5 cm. 1888. Chicago, Art Institute (Coburn Memorial Collection)

12. *Still Life with Three Puppies.* 91·8 × 62·6 cm. 1888. New York, Museum of Modern Art (Mrs. Simon Guggenheim Fund)

13. *Van Gogh Painting Sunflowers.* 73 × 92 cm. 1888. Amsterdam, Van Gogh Foundation

14. *Night Café at Arles* (*Mme Ginoux*). 72 × 92 cm. 1888. Moscow, Museum of Western Art

15. *Vintage at Arles* or *Human Anguish.* 73 × 92 cm. 1888. Copenhagen, Ordrupgaard Museum (Wilhelm Hansen Collection)

16. *Christ in the Garden of Olives.* 73 × 92 cm. 1889. West Palm Beach, Norton Gallery

17. *Bonjour M. Gauguin.* 75 × 55 cm. 1889. Prague, National Gallery

18. *Caricature Self Portrait.* 79·2 × 51·3 cm. 1889. Washington, D.C., National Gallery of Art (Chester Dale Collection)

19. *Caribbean Woman with Sunflowers.* 64 × 54 cm. 1889. New York, Dr. and Mrs. Harry Bakwin

20. *Yellow Christ.* 92 × 73·5 cm. 1889. Buffalo, Albright-Knox Art Gallery

21. *Green Christ* or *Breton Calvary.* 92 × 73 cm. 1889. Brussels, Musées Royaux des Beaux-Arts de Belgique

22. *Breton Girls by the Sea.* 92 × 73 cm. 1889. Tokyo, National Museum of Western Art

23. *The Seaweed Harvesters.* 87 × 122·5 cm. 1889. Essen, Folkwang Museum

24. *The Ham.* 50 × 58 cm. 1889? Washington, D.C., Phillips Collection

25. *Loss of Virginity.* 90 × 130 cm. 1890. Provincetown, Walter P. Chrysler, Jr.

26. *Vahine No Te Tiare. Woman with a Flower.* 70 × 46 cm. 1891. Copenhagen, Ny Carlsberg Glyptothek

27. *Self Portrait with Palette.* 55 × 46 cm. 1893. Los Angeles, Mr. and Mrs. Norton Simon

28. *The Meal* or *The Bananas.* 73 × 92 cm. 1891. Paris, Louvre

29. *Reverie* or *The Woman in the Red Dress.* 92 × 73 cm. 1891. Kansas City, Atkins Museum, Nelson Gallery (Nelson Fund)

30. *Nafea Faaipoipo. When will You Marry?* 101·5 × 77·5 cm. 1892. Basle, Kunstmuseum

31. *Manao Tupapau. The Spirit of the Dead Keeps Watch.* 73 × 92 cm. 1892. Buffalo, Albright-Knox Art Gallery (A. Conger Goodyear Collection)

32. *Ia Orana Maria. Hail Mary.* 113·7 × 87·7 cm. 1891. New York, Metropolitan Museum of Art

33. *Ta Matete. The Market.* 73 × 91·5 cm. 1892. Basle, Kunstmuseum

34. *Pastorales Tahitiennes.* 86 × 113 cm. 1893. Leningrad, Hermitage

35. *Fatata Te Miti. Near the Sea.* 67·9 × 91·5 cm. 1892. Washington, D.C., National Gallery of Art (Chester Dale Collection)

36. Detail from *Fatata Te Miti. Near the Sea* (Plate 35)

37. *Ea Haere Ia Oe. Go!* 92 × 73 cm. 1893. Leningrad, Hermitage

38. *Mahana No Atua. The Day of God.* 69·6 × 89·9 cm. 1894. Chicago, Art Institute (Helen Birch Bartlett Collection)

39. *Hina Tefatou. The Moon Goddess and the Earth Genie.* 114·3 × 62·2 cm. 1893. New York, Museum of Modern Art (Lillie P. Bliss Collection)

40. *Aita Parari Te Tamari Vahine Judith* or *Annah the Javanese.* 116 × 81 cm. 1893. Berne, Private Collection

41. *Nevermore.* 59·5 × 117 cm. 1897. London, Courtauld Institute Galleries

42. *Village Under Snow.* 62 × 87 cm. 1894? Paris, Louvre

43. *The White Horse.* 140 × 91 cm. 1898. Paris, Louvre

44. Detail from *Where Do We Come From? What Are We? Where Are We Going?* 139 × 374·5 cm. 1897. Boston, Museum of Fine Arts (Arthur Gordon Tompkins Residuary Fund)

45. Detail from *Where Do We Come From? What Are We? Where Are We Going?* 139 × 374·5 cm. 1897. Boston, Museum of Fine Arts (Arthur Gordon Tompkins Residuary Fund)

46. *Girl with Fan.* 91 × 73 cm. 1902. Essen, Folkwang Museum

47. *Woman and Two Children.* 97·2 × 74·3 cm. 1901. Chicago, Art Institute (Helen Birch Bartlett Collection)

48. *Contes Barbares.* 130 × 91·5 cm. 1902. Essen, Folkwang Museum

1. *GAUGUIN AT HIS EASEL.* 1885. Berne, Dr. Jacques Koerfer

2. *INTERIOR OF THE ARTIST'S HOME IN PARIS, RUE CARCEL.* 1881. Oslo,
National Gallery

3. *THE SNOW, RUE CARCEL.* 1883. Copenhagen, Madame Eva Kiaer

4. *STILL LIFE WITH HORSE'S HEAD*. 1885. Paris, Private Collection

5. *STILL LIFE WITH THE PROFILE OF LAVAL.* 1886. Mrs. Walter B. Ford II

6. *THE BEACH AT DIEPPE.* 1885. Copenhagen, Ny Carlsberg Glyptotek

7. *THE DANCE OF THE FOUR BRETON GIRLS.* 1886. Munich, Bayerische
Staatsgemäldesammlungen

8. *THE BATHERS.* 1887. Buenos Aires, Di Tella Collection

9. *TROPICAL VEGETATION, MARTINIQUE*. 1887. Edinburgh, National Gallery of Scotland

13. *VAN GOGH PAINTING SUNFLOWERS*. 1888. Amsterdam, Van Gogh Foundation

12. *STILL LIFE WITH THREE PUPPIES*. 1888. New York, Museum of Modern Art
(Mrs. Simon Guggenheim Fund)

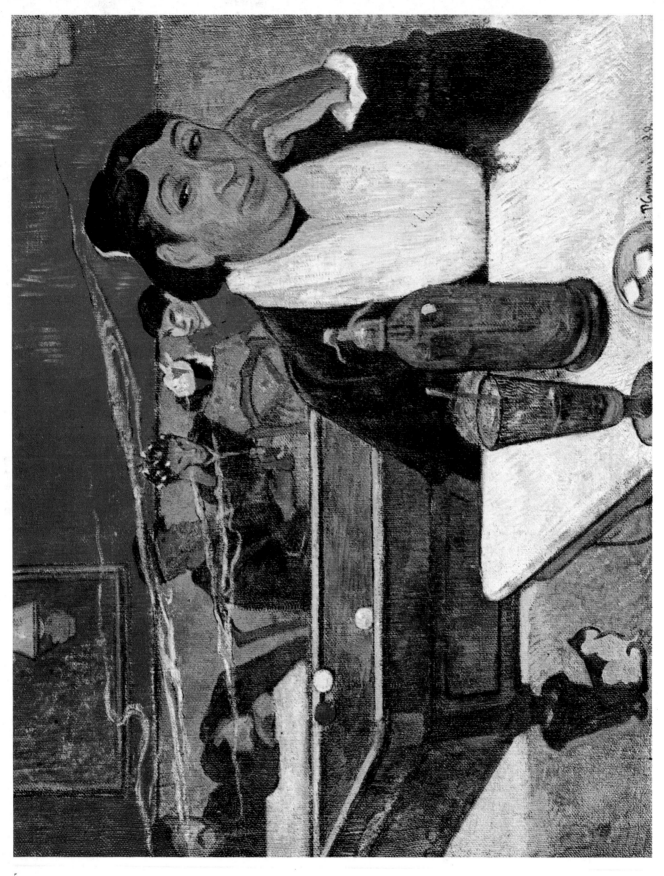

14. *NIGHT CAFE AT
ARLES (MME
GINOUX)*. 1888.
Moscow, Museum of
Western Art

15. *VINTAGE AT ARLES* or *HUMAN ANGUISH*. 1888. Copenhagen, Ordrupgaard Museum (Wilhelm Hansen Collection)

16. *CHRIST IN THE GARDEN OF OLIVES.* 1889. West Palm Beach, Norton Gallery

17. *BONJOUR M. GAUGUIN.* 1889. Prague, National Gallery

18. *CARICATURE SELF PORTRAIT*. 1889. Washington, D.C., National Gallery of Art
(Chester Dale Collection)

19. *CARIBBEAN WOMAN WITH SUNFLOWERS.* 1889. New York, Dr. and Mrs. Harry Bakwin

20. *YELLOW CHRIST.* 1889. Buffalo, Albright-Knox Art Gallery

21. *GREEN CHRIST* or *BRETON CALVARY*. 1889. Brussels, Musées Royaux des Beaux-Arts de Belgique

23. *THE SEAWEED HARVESTERS.* 1889. Essen, Folkwang Museum

22. *BRETON GIRLS BY THE SEA.* 1880. Tokyo, National Museum of Western Art

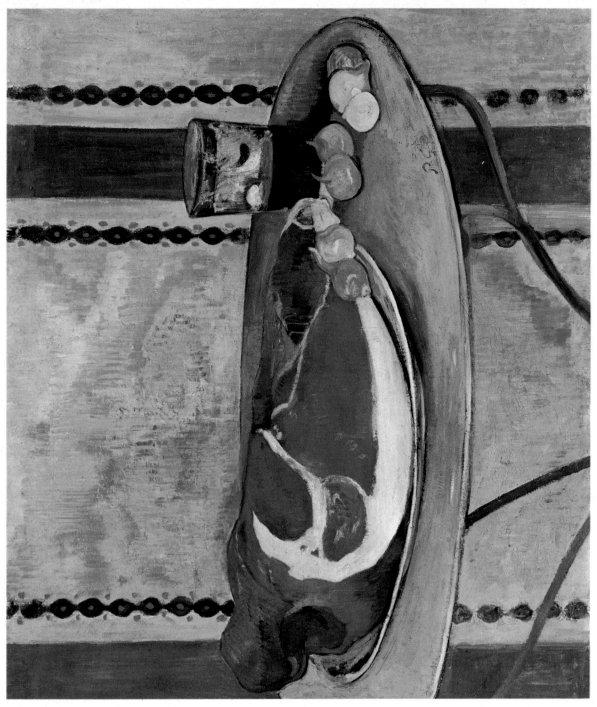

24. *THE HAM.* 1889? Washington, D.C., Phillips Collection

25. *LOSS OF VIRGINITY.* 1890. Provincetown, Walter P. Chrysler, Jr.

26. *VAHINE NO TE TIARE. WOMAN WITH A FLOWER.* 1891.
Copenhagen, Ny Carlsberg Glyptothek

27. *SELF PORTRAIT WITH PALETTE.* 1893. Los Angeles, Mr. & Mrs. Norton Simon

28. *THE MEAL* or *THE BANANAS*. 1891. Paris, Louvre

29. *REVERIE* or *THE WOMAN IN THE RED DRESS*. 1891. Kansas City, Atkins Museum, Nelson Gallery (Nelson Fund)

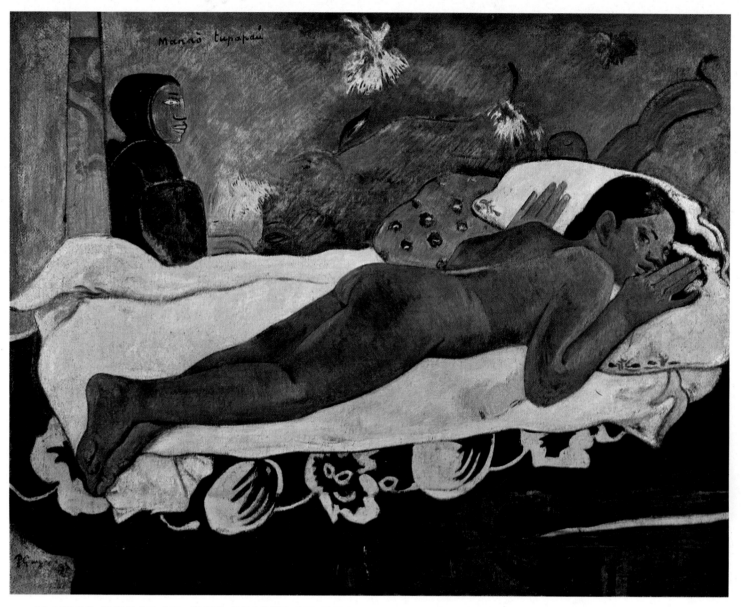

31. *MANAO TUPAPAU. THE SPIRIT OF THE DEAD KEEPS WATCH.* 1892. Buffalo, Albright-Knox Art Gallery (A. Conger Goodyear Collection)

30. *NAFEA FAAIPOIPO. WHEN WILL YOU MARRY?* 1892. Basle, Kunstmuseum

IA ORANA MARIA

32. *IA ORANA MARIA. HAIL MARY.*
1891. New York, Metropolitan Museum of Art

33. *TA MATETE. THE MARKET.* 1892.
Basle, Kunstmuseum

34. *PASTORALES TAHITIENNES.* 1893. Leningrad, Hermitage

35. *FATATA TE MITI. NEAR THE SEA.* 1892. Washington, National Gallery of Art (Chester Dale Collection)

36. Detail from *FATATA TE MITI. NEAR THE SEA* (Plate 35)

37. *EA HAERE IA OE. GO!* 1893. Leningrad, Hermitage

38. *MAHANA NO ATUA. THE DAY OF GOD.* 1894. Chicago, Art Institute (Helen Birch
Bartlett Collection)

39. *HINA TEFATOU. THE MOON GODDESS AND THE EARTH GENIE.* 1893. New
York, Museum of Modern Art (Lillie P. Bliss Collection)

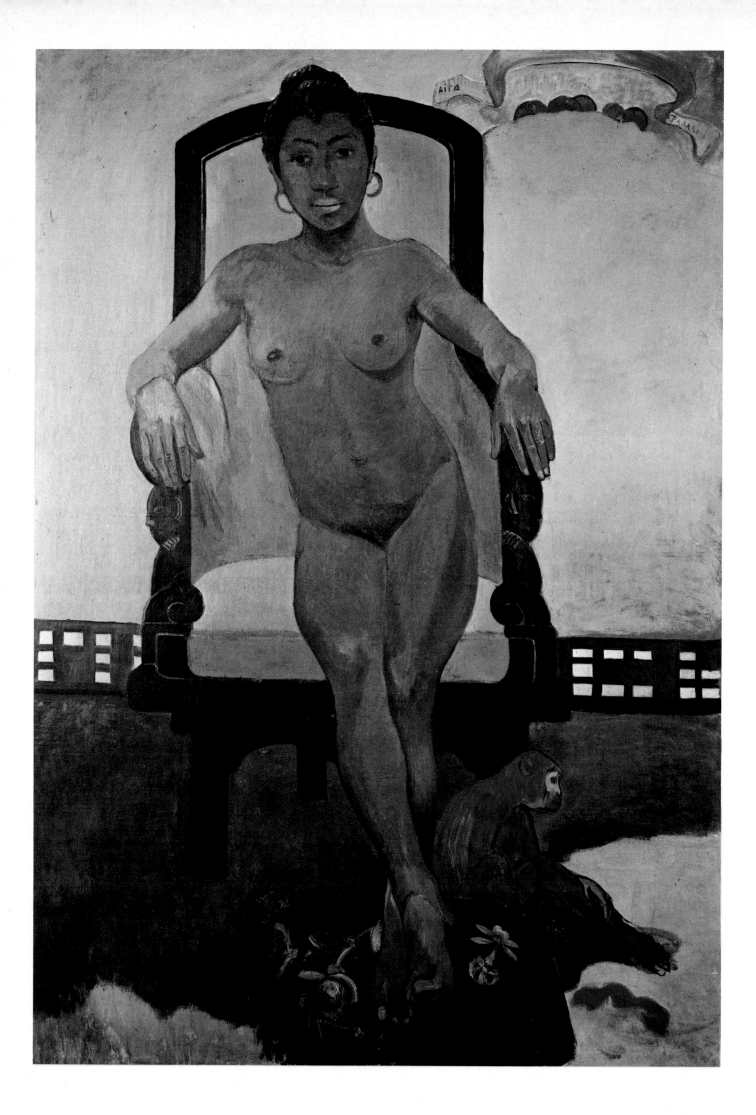

41. *NEVERMORE.* 1897. London, Courtauld Institute Galleries

40. *AITA PARARI TE TAMARI VAHINE JUDITH* or *ANNAH THE JAVANESE.*
1893. Berne, Private Collection

42. *VILLAGE UNDER SNOW.* 1894? Paris, Louvre

43. *THE WHITE HORSE.* 1898. Paris, Louvre

44. Detail from *WHERE DO WE COME FROM? WHAT ARE WE? WHERE ARE WE GOING?* 1897. Boston, Museum of Fine Arts (Arthur Gordon Tompkins Residuary Fund)

45. Detail from *WHERE DO WE COME FROM? WHAT ARE WE? WHERE ARE WE GOING?* 1897. Boston, Museum of Fine Arts (Arthur Gordon Tompkins Residuary Fund)

46. *GIRL WITH FAN.* 1902. Essen, Folkwang Museum

47. *WOMAN AND TWO CHILDREN*. 1901. Chicago, Art Institute (Helen Birch Bartlett Collection)

48. *CONTES BARBARES.* 1902. Essen, Folkwang Museum